# Christianity: HOAX or HISTORY?

## JOSH McDOWELL

POCKET GUIDES™
Tyndale House Publishers, Inc.
Wheaton, Illinois

Unless otherwise noted, all Scripture quotations are taken from
*The Living Bible*, copyright © 1971 owned by assignment by KNT
Charitable Trust.

Excerpts from Josh McDowell's *Evidence That Demands a Verdict*
(San Bernardino, Calif.: Here's Life Publishers, 1979) are used by
permission.

Edited by Dave and Neta Jackson

Pocket Guide is a trademark of Tyndale House Publishers, Inc.

Library of Congress Catalog Card Number 89-50079
ISBN 0-8423-0367-7
Copyright © 1989 by Josh McDowell
All rights reserved
Printed in the United States of America

**99   98   97   96   95**
12   11   10   9   8   7

# CONTENTS

# He Changed My Life

Thomas Aquinas wrote: "There is within every soul a thirst for happiness and meaning."

I wanted to be happy. There's nothing wrong with that. I also wanted to find meaning in life. I wanted answers to the questions: Who am I? Why in the world am I here? Where am I going?

More than that, I wanted to be free. Freedom to me was not going out and doing what I wanted to do. Freedom was having the power to do what I knew I ought to do . . . but didn't have the power to do.

So I started looking for answers. It seemed that almost everyone was into some sort of religion, so I did the obvious thing and took off for church.

I must have found the wrong church, though. Some of you know what I mean: I felt worse inside the church than I did outside.

I've always been very practical, and when one thing doesn't work, I chuck it.

So I chucked religion. The only thing I had ever gotten out of religion was the change I took out of the offering to buy a milkshake. And that's about all many people ever gain from "religion."

I began to wonder if prestige was the answer. So in college I ran for freshman class president and got elected. It was neat knowing everyone on campus, having everyone say, "Hi, Josh," making the decisions, spending the university's money and the students' money to get speakers I wanted. It was great, but it wore off like everything else I had tried.

I was like a boat out in the ocean being tossed back and forth by the waves, the circumstances. And I couldn't find anyone who could tell me how to live differently *or* give me the strength to do it.

Then I began to notice people who seemed to be riding above the circumstances of university life. One important thing I noticed was that they seemed to possess an inner, constant source of joy— a state of mind not dependent on their surroundings. They were disgustingly happy. They had something I didn't have . . . and I wanted it.

I began purposely to spend more time with these people, and we ended up sitting around a table in the student union one afternoon. Finally, I leaned back in my chair and said, "Tell me, have you always been this way, or has something changed your lives? Why are you so different from the other students, the leaders on campus, the professors? Why?"

One student looked me straight in the eye—with a little smile—and said two words I never thought I'd hear as part of any solution in a university. She said, "Jesus Christ."

I said, "Oh, for God's sake, don't give me that garbage. I'm fed up with religion; I'm fed up with the church. Don't give me that garbage about religion."

She shot back, "Mister, I didn't say 'religion'; I said, 'Jesus Christ.'"

It wasn't long before these new friends challenged me intellectually to examine the claims that Jesus Christ is God's Son, that He took on human flesh, that He lived among real men and women and died on the cross for the sins of mankind, that He was buried, and that He arose three days later and could change a person's life in the twentieth century.

Finally, I accepted their challenge. I did it out of pride, to refute them. But I didn't know there were facts. I didn't know there was evidence that a person could evaluate.

As I delved into my research on Christ, I discovered that men and women down through the ages have been divided over the question "Who is Jesus?"

It didn't take long for the people who knew Jesus to realize that He was making astounding claims about Himself. Especially during the trial of Jesus—the trial that eventually led Him to the cross—I found one of the clearest references to Jesus' claims of deity.

Then the High Priest asked him. "Are you the Messiah, the Son of God?"

Jesus said, "I am, and you will see me sitting at the right hand of God, and returning to earth in the clouds of heaven" (Mark 14:61-62).

Jesus claimed to be God. He didn't leave any other option open. His claim must either be true or false. Jesus' question to His disciples, "Who do *you* think I am?" (Matthew 16:15) has several alternatives.

WAS HE A LIAR?

If, when Jesus made His claims, He knew that He was not God, then He was lying and deliberately deceiving His followers. And if He was a liar, then He was also a hypocrite because He told others to be honest, whatever the cost, while He Himself taught and lived a colossal lie.

This view of Jesus, however, doesn't coincide with what we know either of Him or of the results of His life and teachings. Whenever Jesus has been proclaimed, lives have been changed for the good, nations have been changed for the better. Thieves have been made honest, alcoholics have been cured, hateful individuals have become channels of love, unjust persons have become just.

William Lecky, one of Great Britain's most noted historians and a dedicated opponent of organized Christianity, wrote about Jesus' ministry: "The simple record of these three short years of active life has done more to regenerate and soften mankind than all the discourses of philosophers and all the exhortations of moralists."[1]

Someone who lived as Jesus lived, taught as Jesus taught, and died as Jesus died could not have been a liar. What other alternatives are there?


## WAS HE A LUNATIC?

If it is inconceivable for Jesus to be a liar, then couldn't He actually have thought Himself to be God but been mistaken? After all, it's possible to be sincere and wrong.

Someone who believes he is God sounds like someone today believing himself to be Napoleon. He would be deluded and self-deceived and probably would be locked up so he wouldn't hurt himself or anyone else. Yet, in Jesus we don't observe the abnormalities and imbalance that usually go along with being deranged. His poise and composure when confronted by His enemies would certainly be amazing if He were insane.

Here is a man who spoke some of the most profound sayings ever recorded. His instructions have liberated many individuals in mental bondage.

A student at a California university told me that his psychology professor had said in class that "all he has to do is pick up the Bible and read portions of Christ's teachings to many of his patients. That's all the counseling they need."

Psychiatrist J. T. Fisher, speaking of Jesus' popular "Sermon on the Mount" (Matthew 5–7), says this: "For nearly two thousand years the Christian world has been holding in its hands the complete answer to its restlessness and fruitless yearnings. Here . . . rests the blueprint for successful human life with optimism, mental health, and contentment."[2]


## WAS HE LORD?

I cannot personally conclude that Jesus was a liar or a lunatic. The only other alternative is that He is the Christ—the Son of God—as He claimed to be.

When I discuss this with many people, it's interesting how they respond. I share with them the claims Jesus made about Himself and then the material about Jesus being a liar, lunatic, or Lord. When I ask if they believe Jesus was a liar, there is usually a sharp, "No!"

Then I ask, "Do you believe He was a lunatic?"

The reply is, "Of course not."

Then, "Do you believe He is God?"

But before I can get a breath in edgewise, there is a resounding, "Absolutely not."

Yet, one has only so many choices. One of these options must be true.

The issue with these three alternatives is not *which is possible?* for it is obvious that any of the three could have been possible. But, rather, it is the question *Which is more probable?*

Who you decide Jesus Christ is must not be an idle intellectual exercise. You cannot put Him on the shelf while calling Him a great moral teacher. That is not a valid option because if He was so great and moral, what are you going to do with His claim to be God?

If He was a liar or lunatic, then He can't qualify as a great moral teacher. And if He was a great moral teacher, then He is much more as well. He is either a liar, a lunatic, or the Lord God. You must make a choice.

"But," as the Apostle John wrote, "these are recorded so that you will believe that he is the Messiah, the Son of God, and [more important] that believing in him you will have life" (John 20:31).

Two issues became clear in my study of Christianity:

1. Is Christ's resurrection historically credible? This is crucial because Christ appealed to His resurrection as the proof that His claims of deity were true.

2. Most of what we know about Christ

comes from the New Testament. So, is the New Testament account of Christ reliable—can it be trusted?

These are the questions that I want to address in the remainder of this book.

# *Back from the Grave*

For centuries many of the world's most distinguished philosophers have assaulted Christianity as being irrational, superstitious, and absurd. Many have chosen simply to ignore the central issue of the Resurrection. Others have tried to explain it away through various theories. But the historical evidence just can't be discounted. Confronting the facts of the empty tomb is as convincing today as it was 2,000 years ago.

## A QUESTION OF HISTORY

A student at the University of Uruguay said to me: "Professor McDowell, why can't you refute Christianity?"

"For a very simple reason," I answered. "I am not able to explain away an event in history—the resurrection of Jesus Christ."

How can we explain the empty tomb? Can it possibly be accounted for by any natural cause? Here are some of the facts relevant to the Resurrection:

- Jesus of Nazareth, a Jewish prophet who claimed to be the Christ prophesied in the Jewish Scriptures, was arrested, was judged a political criminal, and was executed by Roman crucifixion.
- Three days after His death and burial, some women who went to His tomb found the body gone.
- In subsequent weeks His disciples claimed that God had raised Him from the dead and that He appeared to them at various times before ascending into heaven.
- From that foundation, Christianity spread throughout the Roman Empire and has continued to exert great influence down through the centuries.

Did the Resurrection actually happen? Was the tomb of Jesus really empty? Those questions raise controversy even today.

After more than 1,000 hours of studying this subject, I have come to the conclusion that the resurrection of Jesus Christ is either one of the most wicked, vicious, heartless hoaxes ever foisted on the minds of human beings—or it is the most remarkable fact of history. The Resurrection issue takes the question "Is Christianity valid?" out of the realm of philosophy and forces it to be a question of history.

Does Christianity have a historically acceptable basis? Is sufficient evidence available to warrant belief in the Resurrection?

## IS THE NEW TESTAMENT RELIABLE?

Because the New Testament provides the primary historical source for information on the Resurrection, many critics during the nineteenth century attacked the reliability of these biblical documents.

By the end of the nineteenth century, however, archaeological discoveries had confirmed the accuracy of the New Testament manuscripts; many places, events, and people referred to in the New Testament turned out to be true. Discoveries of early papyri manuscripts have also helped bridge the gap between the time of Christ and existing manuscripts from a later date.

Those findings increased scholarly confidence in the reliability of the Bible. William F. Albright, who in his day was the world's foremost biblical archaeologist, said: "We can already say emphatically that there is no longer any solid basis for dating any book of the New Testament after about A.D. 80—two full generations before the date between 130 and 150 given by the more radical New Testament critics of today."[1]

Coinciding with the papyri discoveries, an abundance of other manuscripts came to light. (More than 24,000 copies of early New Testament manuscripts are known to be in existence today.) That fact motivated Sir Frederick Kenyon, one of the leading authorities on the reliability of ancient manuscripts, to write:

> The interval then between the dates of original composition and the earliest extant evidence becomes so small as to be in fact negligible, and the last foundation for any doubt that the Scriptures have come down to us substantially as they were written has now been removed. Both the authenticity and the general integrity of the books of the New Testament may be regarded as finally established.[2]

The historian Luke wrote of "authentic evidence" concerning the Resurrection. Sir William Ramsey, who attempted for fifteen years to undermine Luke's credentials as a historian and to refute the New Testament's reliability, finally concluded: "Luke is a historian of the first rank. . . . This author should be placed along with the very greatest of historians."[3]

## LIVING WITNESSES
The New Testament accounts of the Resurrection were being circulated within the lifetimes of men and women alive at the time of the event. Those people could certainly have confirmed or denied the accuracy of such accounts.

The writers of the four Gospels either

had themselves been witnesses or else were relating the accounts of eyewitnesses of the actual events. In advocating their case for the gospel, a word that means "good news," the apostles appealed (even when confronting their most severe opponents) to common knowledge concerning the facts of the Resurrection. (See chapter 3.)

F. F. Bruce, professor of biblical criticism and exegesis at the University of Manchester, says concerning the value of the New Testament records as primary sources: "Had there been any tendency to depart from the facts in any material respect, the possible presence of hostile witnesses in the audience would have served as a further corrective."[4]

The facts and details of what Christ had said and done were presented in the very presence of antagonistic eyewitnesses of Christ who knew the events surrounding Christ's life and ministry. In that you have historically what we call today in a court of law the principle of "cross-examination" to discern truth from fabrication.


BACKGROUND

The New Testament witnesses were fully aware of the background against which the Resurrection took place. The body of Jesus, in accordance with Jewish burial custom, was wrapped in a linen cloth. About 100 pounds of aromatic spices, mixed together to form a gummy or cement-like substance, were applied to the wrappings of cloth about the body to form an encasement weighing about 120 pounds.

After the body was placed in a solid rock tomb, the historical account points out that an extremely large stone closed the entrance of the tomb. The large stone weighed approximately one-and-a-half to two tons and was rolled (by means of levers) against the tomb's entrance.

A Roman guard unit of sixteen strictly disciplined fighting men was stationed to guard the tomb. This guard unit affixed on the tomb the Roman seal, which was meant to prevent any attempt at vandalizing the sepulcher. Anyone trying to move the stone from the tomb's entrance would have broken the seal and incurred the wrath of Roman law.

But three days later the tomb was empty. The followers of Jesus said He had risen from the dead. They reported that He appeared to them during a period of forty days, showing Himself to them by many "infallible proofs." Paul the apostle recounted that Jesus appeared to more than 500 of His followers at one time, the majority of whom were still alive and could confirm what Paul wrote. No one acquainted with the facts can accurately say that Jesus appeared to just "an insignificant few."

## ATTEMPTED EXPLANATIONS

Christians believe that Jesus was bodily resurrected in time and space by the supernatural power of God. The difficulties of belief may be great, but the problems inherent in unbelief present even greater difficulties. Put another way, when it comes to the Resurrection, *the burden of unbelief is greater than the burden of belief.*

The theories advanced to explain the Resurrection by "natural causes" are weak; they actually help to build confidence in the truth of the Resurrection.

## THE WRONG TOMB?

A theory propounded by Kirsopp Lake assumes that the women who reported the body was missing had mistakenly gone to the wrong tomb. If so, then the disciples who went to check up on the women's statement must have also gone to the wrong tomb. We may be certain, however, that the Jewish authorities, who asked for a Roman guard to be stationed at the tomb to prevent Jesus' body from being stolen, would not have been mistaken about the location. Nor would the Roman guards, for they were there!

If the Resurrection claim was merely because of a geographical mistake, the Jewish authorities would have lost no time in producing the body from the proper tomb, thus effectively squelching for all time any rumor of resurrection.

But what did the soldiers and the Jewish authorities do? The record states that

some of the guards went into the city and reported to the chief priests everything that had happened. When the chief priests had met with the elders and devised a plan, they gave the soldiers a large sum of money, telling them, "You are to say, 'His disciples came during the night and stole him away while we were asleep.' If this report gets to the governor, we will satisfy him and keep you out of trouble." So the soldiers took the money and did as they were instructed. And this story has been widely circulated among the Jews to this very day.
(Matthew 28:11-15, NIV)

## THE BODY STOLEN?
Consider the theory that the body was stolen by the disciples while the guards slept. As the Scriptures note, this is the very oldest attempted explanation.

However, the depression and cowardice of the disciples provide a hard-hitting argument against their suddenly becoming so brave and daring as to face a detachment of soldiers at the tomb and steal the body. They were in no mood to attempt something like that.

J. N. D. Anderson has been dean of the faculty of law at the University of London and director of its Institute of Advanced

Legal Studies. Commenting on the proposition that the disciples stole Christ's body, he says:

> This would run totally contrary to all we know of them: their ethical teaching, the quality of their lives, their steadfastness in suffering and persecution. Nor would it begin to explain their dramatic transformation from dejected and dispirited escapists into witnesses whom no opposition could muzzle.[5]

An alternative theory that the Jewish or Roman authorities moved Christ's body is no more reasonable an explanation for the empty tomb than theft by the disciples. If the authorities had the body in their possession or knew where it was, why, when the disciples were preaching the Resurrection in Jerusalem, didn't they explain: "Wait! We moved the body. He didn't rise from the grave"?

And if such a rebuttal failed, why didn't they explain exactly where Jesus' body lay? If this failed, why didn't they recover the corpse, put it on a cart, and wheel it through the center of Jerusalem? Such an action would have destroyed Christianity—not in the cradle but in the womb!

Dr. John Warwick Montgomery, an attorney and dean of the Simon Greenleaf School of Law, further explains, "It passes the bounds of credibility that the early Christians could have manufactured such a tale and then preached it among those

# ☞ A Physiologist Looks at the Crucifixion

Samuel Houghton, M.D., the great physiologist from the University of Dublin, relates his view on the physical cause of Christ's death:

"When the soldier pierced with his spear the side of Christ, He was already dead; and the flow of blood and water that followed was either a natural phenomenon explicable by natural causes or it was a miracle. . . .

"Repeated observations and experiments made upon men and animals have led me to the following results—

"When the left side is freely pierced after death by a large knife, comparable in size with a Roman spear, three distinct cases may be noted:

"First. No flow of any kind follows the wound, except a slight trickling of blood.

"Second. A copious flow of blood only follows the wound.

"Third. A flow of water only, succeeded by a few drops of blood, follows the wound.

"Of these three cases, the first is that which usually occurs; the second is found in cases of death by drowning and by strychnia, and may be demonstrated by destroying an animal with that poison, and it can be proved to be the natural case of a crucified person; and the third is found in cases of death from pleurisy, pericarditis, and rupture of the heart.

With the foregoing cases most anatomists who have devoted their attention to this subject are familiar; but the two following cases, although readily explicable on physiological principles, are not recorded in the books (except by St. John). Nor have I been fortunate enough to meet with them.

"Fourth. A copious flow of water, succeeded by a copious flow of blood, follows the wound.

"Fifth. A copious flow of blood, succeeded by a copious flow of water, follows the wound.

". . . Death by crucifixion causes a condition of blood in the lungs similar to that produced by drowning and strychnia; the fourth case would occur in a crucified person who had previously to crucifixion suffered from pleuritic effusion; and the fifth case would occur in a crucified person, who had died upon the cross from rupture of the heart. The history of the days preceding our Lord's crucifixion effectually excludes the supposition of pleurisy, which is also out of the question if blood first and water afterwards followed the wound. There remains, therefore, no supposition possible to explain the recorded phenomenon except *the combination of the crucifixion and the rupture of the heart*.

"That . . . rupture of the heart actually occurred I firmly believe. . . ."

From *Evidence That Demands a Verdict*, 198-199.

who might easily have refuted it simply by producing the body of Jesus."[6]


## HALLUCINATIONS?

One of the most desperate appeals to explain away the Resurrection is the appeal to hallucinations. In no way can one say that Jesus' appearances were stereotyped or that His followers were hallucinating what happened to them according to some trumped-up formula intended to convince people of what was actually not so.

The American Psychiatric Association's official glossary defines a "hallucination as a false sensory perception in the absence of an actual external stimulus."

Hallucinations are linked to an individual's subconscious and to his or her particular past experiences, making it very unlikely that even two people could have the same hallucination at the same time. Christ appeared to many people, and descriptions of the appearance involve great detail, like those which psychologists regard as determined by reality.

Christ also ate with those to whom He appeared. And He not only exhibited His wounds, but He also encouraged a closer inspection. An illusion does not sit down and have dinner with you, and it cannot be scrutinized by various individuals at will.

An hallucination is a very private event—a purely subjective experience void of any external reference or object. If two people cannot initiate or sustain the same vision without any external object or reference, how could more than five hundred do so at one time? This is not only contrary to this principle of hallucinations but also strongly mitigates against it. The many claimed hallucinations would be a far greater miracle than the miracle of resurrection. This is what makes the view that Christ's appearances were hallucinations so ludicrous.


## DID JESUS SWOON?

Another theory was popularized by Venturini several centuries ago and is often quoted today. This is the swoon theory, which says that Jesus didn't die; he merely fainted from exhaustion and loss of blood. Everyone thought He was dead, but later He resuscitated and the disciples thought it to be a resurrection.

Skeptic David Friedrich Strauss—certainly no believer in the Resurrection—gave the deathblow to any thought that Jesus revived from a swoon:

> It is impossible that a being who had stolen half-dead out of the sepulcher, who crept about weak and ill, wanting medical treatment, who required bandaging, strengthening and indulgence, and who still at last yielded to His sufferings, could have given to the disciples the impression that He was a Conqueror over death and the grave, the Prince of

Life, an impression which lay at the bottom of their future ministry. Such a resuscitation could only have weakened the impression which He had made upon them in life and in death, at the most could only have given it an elegiac voice, but could by no possibility have changed their sorrow into enthusiasm, have elevated their reverence into worship.[7]

André Kole is considered one of the world's leading illusionists, often called the magician's magician. He has never been fooled by another illusionist or magician. He has created and sold more than 1,400 illusionary and magical effects.

When André was a student, he studied psychology. He was challenged to apply his proficiency to the Resurrection, to explain it away by modern magic and illusion. He accepted the challenge—but concluded that there is no way through modern illusionary effects or magic that Jesus could have deceived His followers.

Once, when discussing this with me, he said, "Josh, there are too many built-in safety factors." Consider the weight of the two-ton stone rolled against the tomb, the fear of death for the Roman guards if they failed in their duty, the physical state of a crucified man, to name a few.

Kole was forced to the conclusion that if the Resurrection was a lie, the disciples must have known it was a lie.

## DECEIT BY THE DISCIPLES?

If the disciples lied about the Resurrection, then they died for a lie.

Good historical tradition shows us twelve Jewish men, eleven of whom died martyrs' deaths as a tribute to one thing: an empty tomb and the appearances of Jesus of Nazareth alive after His death by crucifixion.

Remember that at first the disciples didn't believe it either—not until they saw Him with their own eyes. For forty days after His resurrection, these men walked with Jesus, lived with Him, ate with Him. His resurrection was accompanied by many "convincing proofs" (Acts 1:3).

While it's true that thousands of people throughout history have died for a lie, they did so *only* if they thought it to be the truth.

Tertullian said, "No man would be willing to die unless he knew he had the truth."[8]

What happened to these disciples of Jesus? Dr. Michael Green points out that "the Resurrection was the belief that turned brokenhearted followers of a crucified rabbi into the courageous witness and martyrs of the early church. . . . You could imprison them, flog them, but you could not make them deny their conviction that 'on the third day, he rose again.'"[9]

# Consider the Facts

So many security precautions were taken with the trial, crucifixion, burial, entombment, sealing, and guarding of Christ's tomb that it becomes very difficult for critics to defend their position that Christ did not rise from the dead.

## FACT #1: BROKEN ROMAN SEAL

The first obvious fact is the breaking of the seal that stood for the power and authority of the Roman Empire. The consequences of breaking the seal were extremely severe.

Once the seal was violated, the "FBI" of the Roman Empire was called into action to find the person or persons who were responsible. If they were apprehended, it meant automatic execution by crucifixion upside down (where your guts ran into your throat). People feared the breaking of the seal.

The disciples after the crucifixion of Jesus were an unlikely group to risk such an act. They were afraid for their lives. Remember that even before the Crucifixion, when Jesus was arrested in the Garden of Gethsemane, they left Him and ran away. Peter denied that he knew Jesus three times in one night. Only John and some of the women were with Jesus when He died. They spent the next few days behind closed doors "for fear of the Jews" (John 20:19).

## FACT #2: EMPTY TOMB

Another obvious fact was the empty tomb.

The disciples of Jesus did not flee to Athens or Rome to preach that Christ was raised from the dead. Rather, they went right back to Jerusalem, where, if their claims were false, the falsity would be evident.

The empty tomb was "too notorious to be denied." The burial site was well known not only to Christians and Jews but also to the Romans. This is why Dr. Paul Althaus states that the Resurrection "could not have been maintained in Jerusalem for a single day, for a single hour, if the emptiness of the tomb had not been established as a fact for all concerned."[1]

Both Jewish and Roman sources and traditions admit an empty tomb. Those sources range from Josephus to a compilation of fifth-century Jewish writings called the *Toledoth Jeshu.* Even the Jewish leaders acknowledged that the tomb was empty. Dr. Paul Maier calls this "positive evidence from a hostile source, which is the strongest kind of historical evidence. In essence, this means that if a source admits a fact decidedly not in its favor, then that fact is genuine."

Please keep in mind that the earliest Jewish reaction to the proclamation of Christ's resurrection was an aggressive attempt to *explain away* the empty tomb, not deny that it was empty.

Dr. Ron Sider puts it this way: "If the Christians and their Jewish opponents both agree that the tomb was empty, we have little choice but to accept the empty tomb as historical fact."

Dr. Maier observes that "if all the evidence is weighed carefully and fairly, it is indeed justifiable, according to the canons of historical research, to conclude that the sepulcher of Joseph of Arimathea, in which Jesus was buried, was actually empty on the morning of the first Easter. And no shred of evidence has yet been discovered in literary sources, epigraphy, or archaeology that would disprove this statement." Dr. D. H. Van Daalen concludes that "it is extremely difficult to object to the empty tomb on historical grounds."

FACT #3: LARGE STONE MOVED
On that Sunday morning the first thing that impressed the people who ap-

proached the tomb was the unusual position of the one-and-a-half- to two-ton stone that had been lodged in front of the doorway. All the Gospel writers mention it: The stone had been rolled away—not just away from the entrance to the tomb, but away from the tomb itself.

Now, I ask you, if the disciples had wanted to tiptoe around the sleeping guards, roll the stone away, and steal Jesus' body, how could they have done that without the guards' awareness? Those soldiers, even if asleep, would have to have had cotton in their ears, with earmuffs on, along with a heavy dose of knockout pills, not to have heard that huge stone being moved.


FACT #4: ROMAN GUARD
GOES AWOL

The Roman guards fled. They left their place of responsibility. How can their dereliction of duty be explained, when Roman military discipline was so exceptional?

The Justinian Code, compiled in the sixth century, mentions in *Digest No.49* all the offenses that required the death penalty under Roman law. The fear of their superiors' wrath and the possibility of death meant that Roman soldiers paid close attention to the most minute details of their job. Falling asleep on duty, leaving one's position, and failing in any way resulted in severe discipline.

One way a guard was put to death was by being stripped of his clothes and then burned alive with a fire started with his garments. If it was not apparent which soldier had failed in his duty, then lots were drawn to see which one would be punished with death for the guard unit's failure.

Certainly the entire unit would not have fallen asleep with that kind of threat over their heads. Dr. George Currie, a student of Roman military discipline, wrote that fear of punishment "produced flawless attention to duty, especially in the night watches."[2]

Dr. Bill White is in charge of the Garden Tomb in Jerusalem. His responsibilities have caused him to study the Resurrection and subsequent events. Dr. White makes several observations about the fact that the Jewish authorities bribed the Roman guards to say that Jesus' disciples had stolen His body:

> If the stone were simply rolled to one side of the tomb, as would be necessary to enter it, then they might be justified in accusing the men of sleeping at their posts, and in punishing them severely. If the men protested that the earthquake broke the seal and that the stone rolled back under the vibration, they would still be liable to punishment for behavior that might be labeled cowardice. But these possibilities do not meet the case. There was some undeniable evidence

which made it impossible for the chief priests to bring any charges against the guard. The Jewish authorities must have visited the scene, examined the stone, and recognized its position as making it humanly impossible for their men to have permitted its removal. No twist of ingenuity could provide an adequate answer or a scapegoat, and so they were forced to bribe the guard and seek to hush things up.

## FACT #5: GRAVE CLOTHES TELL A TALE

In a literal sense, against all reports to the contrary, the tomb was not totally empty—because of an amazing phenomenon.

After visiting the grave and seeing the stone rolled away, the women ran back and told the disciples. Then Peter and John took off running. John outran Peter and upon arriving at the tomb did not enter. Instead, he leaned over, looked in, and saw something so startling that he immediately believed.

He looked over to the place where the body of Jesus had lain, and there were the grave clothes, in the form of the body, slightly caved in and empty—like the empty chrysalis of a caterpillar's cocoon. That's enough to make a believer out of anybody. John never did get over it.

The first thing that stuck in the minds of the disciples was not the empty tomb but the empty grave clothes.

# FACT #6: JESUS' APPEARANCES CONFIRMED

Christ appeared on several occasions after the cataclysmic events of that first Easter.

When studying an event in history, it is important to know whether enough people who were participants or eyewitnesses to the event were alive when the facts about the event were published. To know this is obviously helpful in ascertaining the accuracy of the published report.

If the number of eyewitnesses is substantial, the event can be regarded as fairly well established. For instance, if we all witness a murder, and a later police report turns out to be a fabrication of lies, we, as eyewitnesses, can refute it.

*More than 500 witnesses.* Several important factors are often overlooked when considering Christ's post-resurrection appearances to individuals. The first is the large number of witnesses who saw Him after that resurrection morning.

One of the earliest records of Christ's appearing after the Resurrection is by Paul in his letter to the Corinthians. The apostle appealed to their knowledge of the fact that Christ had been seen by more than 500 people at one time. Remember, as Paul emphasized, the majority of those people were still alive and could be questioned.

Dr. Edwin M. Yamauchi, associate professor of history at Miami University in Oxford, Ohio, emphasizes:

What gives a special authority to the list [of witnesses] as historical evidence is the reference to most of the five hundred brethren being still alive. St. Paul says in effect, "If you do not believe me, you can ask them." Such a statement in an admittedly genuine letter written within thirty years of the event is almost as strong evidence as one could hope to get for something that happened nearly two thousand years ago."

Let's take the more than 500 witnesses who saw Jesus alive after His death and burial and place them in a courtroom. Do you realize that if each of those 500 people were to testify for only six minutes, including cross examination, you would have an amazing fifty hours of firsthand testimony? Add to this the testimony of many other eyewitnesses and you could well have the largest and most lopsided trial in history.

*Variety of witnesses.* Another factor often overlooked is the variety of situations and people to whom Jesus appeared.

Merrill C. Tenney, former professor at Wheaton College, writes:

It is noteworthy that these appearances are not stereotyped. No two of them are exactly alike. The appearance to Mary Magdalene occurred in early morning (John 20:1); to the travelers to Emmaus in the afternoon (Luke 24:29); and to the apostles in the evening, probably after dark (Luke 24:36). He appeared to Mary in the open air (John 20:14) [but to the

disciples in a closed room (John 20:19)].
Mary was alone when she saw Him; the
disciples were together in a group; and
Paul records that on one occasion He
appeared to more than five hundred at a
time (1 Corinthians 15:6). The reactions
were also varied. Mary was over-
whelmed with emotion (John 20:16-17);
the disciples were frightened (Luke
24:37); Thomas was obstinately incred-
ulous when told of the Lord's resurrection (John 20:25), but worshiped Him
when He manifested Himself. Each occasion had its own peculiar atmosphere
and characteristics, and revealed some
different quality of the risen Lord.

*Hostile witnesses.* A third factor crucial
to interpreting Christ's appearances is that
He also appeared to those who were hostile or unconvinced.

Over and over again I have read or
heard people comment that Jesus was
seen alive after His death and burial only
by His friends and followers. But that line
of reasoning is so pathetic it hardly de-
serves comment.

No author or informed individual would
regard Saul of Tarsus as being a follower
of Christ. The facts show the exact op-
posite. Saul despised Christ and per-
secuted His followers. It was a
life-shattering experience when Christ appeared to him on the Damascus road. Although he was not at that time a disciple,
he later became the Apostle Paul, one of

the greatest witnesses for the truth of the Resurrection.

Also consider James, the brother of Jesus (not James the apostle and elder brother of John). History indicates that Jesus' brother was anything but a believer (John 7:3-5). Yet James not only became a follower of his brother but also died a martyr's death. What caused that change in his attitude and eventually his life?

According to his presence with the followers of Jesus as mentioned in Acts 1:13, his conversion must have occurred very shortly after Jesus' resurrection. The only historical explanation is what Paul said in 1 Corinthians 15:7—Jesus had appeared to James.

The argument that Christ's appearances were only to followers is an argument for the most part from silence, and arguments from silence can be dangerous. It is correct to say that all to whom Jesus appeared eventually became a follower. This is perhaps the best explanation of the conversion of so many of the Jerusalem priests (Acts 6:7).

THE CONCLUSION
Professor Thomas Arnold, for fourteen years a headmaster of Rugby, author of the famous *History of Rome,* and appointed to the chair of modern history at Oxford, was well acquainted with the value of evidence in determining historical facts.

This great scholar said:

> I have been used for many years to study the histories of other times, and to examine and weigh the evidence of those who have written about them, and I know of no one fact in the history of mankind which is proved by better and fuller evidence of a fair inquirer, than the great sign which God hath given us that Christ died and rose again from the dead.[3]

Brooke Foss Westcott, an English scholar, said:

> Taking all the evidence together, it is not too much to say that there is no historic incident better or more variously supported than the resurrection of Christ. Nothing but the antecedent assumption that it must be false could have suggested the idea of deficiency in the proof of it.

One man who was highly skilled at dealing with evidence was Dr. Simon Greenleaf. He was the famous Royal Professor of Law at Harvard University and succeeded Justice Joseph Story as the Dane Professor of Law in the same university.

Greenleaf examined the value of the historical evidence for the resurrection of Jesus Christ to ascertain the truth. He applied the principles contained in his three-volume treatise on evidences. He came to the conclusion that, according to the laws of legal evidence used in courts of law, there is more evidence for the historical fact of the resurrection of Jesus Christ than for just about any other event in ancient history.

## REAL PROOF: THE DISCIPLES' LIVES

But the most telling testimony of all must be the lives of those early Christians. We must ask ourselves: What caused them to go everywhere telling the message of the risen Christ?

Had there been any visible benefits accruing to them from their efforts—prestige, wealth, increased social status, or material benefits—we might logically attempt to account for their actions, for their wholehearted and total allegiance to this "risen Christ."

As a reward for their efforts, however, those early Christians were beaten, stoned to death, thrown to the lions, tortured, crucified. Every conceivable method was used to stop them from talking.

Yet they were peaceful people. They forced their beliefs on no one. Rather, they laid down their lives as the ultimate proof of their complete confidence in the truth of their message.

It has been rightly said that they went through the test of death to determine their veracity. It is important to remember that initially the disciples didn't believe.

But once convinced—in spite of their doubts—they were never to doubt again that Christ was raised from the dead.

Do you know the odds of twelve men, all knowing something was a lie, not cracking under the torture and pressure to admit their deception?


## AN EXAMPLE OF A CAVE-IN

Charles Colson, of Watergate scandal fame, writes that the Watergate cover-up revealed the true nature of humanity under pressure—the survival instinct. Ironically, his learning as an attorney and his years of experience in politics convinced him that Watergate demonstrates that the resurrection of Christ must be true.

This is how Colson arrived at his conclusion: A "thinly disguised panic began to sweep the plush offices of the stately old building that houses the most influential and powerful men in the world."

Yet he saw that even *"with the most powerful office in the world at stake, a small band of hand-picked loyalists, no more than ten of us, could not hold a conspiracy together for more than two weeks.* Think of the power at our fingertips: A mere command from one of us could mobilize generals and cabinet officers, even armies; we could hire or fire personnel and manage billions in agency budgets."

But yet with all this power, prestige,

and their personal reputations and the luxury of their offices at stake, this group of men could not contain a lie.

However, Colson asks: "Was the pressure really all that great at that point? There had certainly been moral failures, criminal violation, even perjury by some. There was certain to be keen embarrassment; at the worst, some might go to prison, though that possibility was by no means certain. But no one was in grave danger; no one's life was at stake.

"Yet, after just a few weeks," observes Colson, "the natural human instinct for self-preservation was so overwhelming that the conspirators, one by one, deserted their leader, walked away from their cause, turned their backs on the power, prestige, and privileges."

How does all this relate to the Resurrection? One criticism of the veracity of Christ's resurrection is that His twelve disciples conceived a "Passover plot." They secretly stole away the body of Christ and neatly disposed of it, and then to their dying breaths maintained a conspiratorial silence. Colson concludes that

if one is to assail the historicity of the Resurrection and therefore the deity of Christ, *one must conclude that there was a conspiracy—a cover-up if you will—by eleven men with the complicity of up to five hundred others*. To subscribe to this argument, one must also be ready to believe that each disciple was willing to be ostracized by friends and family, live in daily fear of death, endure prisons, live penniless and hungry, sacrifice family, be tortured without mercy, and ultimately die—all without ever once renouncing that Jesus had risen from the dead!

This is why the Watergate experience is so instructive to me. If John Dean and the rest of us were so panic-stricken, not by the prospect of beatings and execution, but by political disgrace and possible prison term, one can only speculate about the emotions of the disciples. Unlike the men in the White House, the disciples were powerless people, abandoned by their leader, homeless in a conquered land. Yet they clung tenaciously to their enormously offensive story that their leader had risen from His ignoble death and was alive—and was the Lord.

The Watergate cover-up reveals, I think, the true nature of humanity. None of the memoirs suggest that anyone went to the prosecutor's office out of such noble notions as putting the Constitution above the president or bringing rascals to justice—or even moral indignation. Instead, *the writings of those involved are consistent recitations of the frailty of men. Even political zealots at the pinnacle of power will save their own necks in the crunch, though it may be at the expense of the one they profess to serve so zealously.* Is it really likely, then, that a deliberate cover-up, a plot to perpetuate a lie about the Resurrection, could have survived the violent persecution of the apostles, the scrutiny of early church councils, the horrendous purge of the first-century believers who were cast by the thousands to the lions for refusing to renounce the Lordship of Christ? Is it not probable that at least one of the apostles would have renounced Christ before being beheaded or stoned? Is it not likely that some "smoking gun" document might have been produced exposing the "Passover plot?" Surely one of the conspirators would have made a deal with the authorities. Government and Sanhedrin probably would have welcomed such a soul with open arms and pocketbooks!

Take it from one who was inside the Watergate web looking out, who saw firsthand how vulnerable a cover-up is: Nothing less than a witness as awesome as the resurrected Christ could have caused those men to maintain to their dying day that Jesus is alive and Lord.

The weight of evidence tells me the apostles were indeed telling the truth.

# *The Record Preserved*

After a "free-speech" outdoors lecture I gave at Arizona State University, a professor accompanied by students from his graduate seminar on world literature approached me and said, "Mr. McDowell, you are basing all your claims about Christ on a second-century document that is obsolete. I showed in class today how the New Testament was written so long after Christ that it could not be accurate in what it recorded."

"Sir," I replied, "your opinions about the New Testament are twenty-five years out of date."

I knew where this professor and his students were coming from. As a university student, I had set out to prove that the New Testament was a collection of myths, half-truths, and outright errors. Instead, I ended up with historical evidence for the Bible's reliability that was overwhelming. If other literature of antiquity had the same historical evidence, no one would question its authenticity and reliability.

"So, who cares?" you say. You do. To one degree or another you have developed an opinion on the reliability of the New Testament and its application to your own life. Maybe you haven't thought much about it and just ignore the implications. Maybe you feel skeptical because it was written a long time ago—what possible relevance could it have today? Maybe all those "miracles"—and to top it off, the Resurrection—disqualify it in your mind for serious study. Or maybe you want to believe, but it seems so full of contradictions.

Are you willing to talk about it and look at the facts? Good. Me, too.

QUESTION 1: *How can the New Testament accurately report the facts about Jesus if it wasn't written until 100 years later?*

Many opinions about the records concerning Jesus are based on the conclusions of F. C. Baur, a German critic. Baur assumed that most of the New Testament Scriptures were not written until late in the second century A.D. He concluded that these writings came basically from myths or legends that had developed during the lengthy interval between the lifetime of Jesus and the time those accounts were set down in writing.

FACT: *Recent archaeological discoveries point to the first-century origin of New Testament manuscripts.* (See chapter 1.)

46

## ☞ A Scholar's Challenge

As "little more than a theological joke," Dr. John Robinson, lecturer at Trinity College, Cambridge, decided to investigate the arguments on the late dating of all the New Testament books. The results stunned him. He said the second century arguments were based on scholarly "sloth," the "tyranny of unexamined assumptions," and "almost willful blindness" by previous critics, and concluded that all the New Testament books, including the Gospel of John, had to have been written before A.D. 64. Robinson then challenged his colleagues to try to prove him wrong. If scholars reopen the question, he is convinced, the results will force "the rewriting of many introductions to—and ultimately, theologies of—the New Testament."[1]

FACT: *There is strong evidence within the New Testament that it was written at an early date.*

The Book of Acts records the missionary activity of the early church and was written as a *sequel* by the same person who wrote the Gospel according to Luke. The Book of Acts ends with the Apostle Paul being alive in Rome. This leads us to believe that it was written before he died, since the other major events of his life were recorded. There is reason to believe that Paul was put to death in Nero's persecution of Christians in A.D. 64, which means the Book of Acts was composed before then.

The death of Christ took place around A.D. 30. If the Book of Acts was written before A.D. 64, then the Gospel of Luke was written sometime in the intervening thirty years.

The early church generally taught that the first Gospel composed was Matthew, which places it still closer to the time of Christ. This evidence leads us to believe that the first three Gospels were composed within thirty years of the time these events occurred, when unfriendly witnesses were still living who could have contradicted the Gospels if they had not been accurate.

QUESTION 2: *But aren't the New Testament stories just a bunch of myths and legends that finally got written down?*

Some critics argue that information about Christ was passed by word of mouth until it was written down in the form of the Gospels. Even though the period was much shorter than previously believed, they conclude that the Gospel accounts took on the forms of tales and myths.

FACT: *The period of oral tradition is not long enough to allow for the development of myths and legends.*

Dr. Simon Kistemaker, who has studied the development of myths and legends wrote: "Normally the accumulation of folklore among people of primitive culture takes many generations; it is a gradual process spread over centuries of time. But . . . we must conclude that the Gospel stories were produced and collected within little more than one generation." Professor A. N. Sherwin-White, a prominent historian of Roman/Greek times, points out that for the New Testament accounts to be legend, the rate of legendary accumulation would have to be unbelievably accelerated; more generations are needed.

QUESTION 3: *How do we know that the Bible we read today is the same as when it was originally written?*

In other words, since we don't have the original documents, how do we know the copies we have are reliable? Accusations abound about zealous monks changing the biblical text as it was copied during the Dark Ages.

FACT: *Although we do not possess originals, copies exist from a very early date.*

When I first wrote *Evidence That Demands a Verdict,* I was able to document 14,000 manuscripts of the New Testament. However, with new discoveries, I can document 24,633 manuscripts of just the New Testament. Altogether there are more than 24,000 New Testament manuscripts and portions thereof in Greek and other early versions!

The significance of this number of

manuscripts documenting the New Testament is even greater when one realizes that in all of ancient history, the second runner-up in terms of manuscript authority is the *Iliad* by Homer—and it has only 643 surviving documents.

FACT: *The time span between the originals and the earliest copies in possession is extremely short.*

The New Testament was originally written in Greek. Though we do not have any originals, there are approximately 5,500

---

## ANCIENT MANUSCRIPTS:

| Author/Work | When Written |
|---|---|
| Caesar | 100–44 B.C. |
| Livy | 59 B.C.–A.D. 17 |
| Plato (*Tetralogies*) | 427–347 B.C. |
| Tacitus (*Annals*) | A.D. 100 |
| Tacitus (*minor works*) | A.D. 100 |
| Pliny the Younger (*History*) | A.D. 61–113 |
| Thucydides (*History*) | 460–400 B.C. |
| Suetonius (*De Vita Caesarum*) | A.D. 75–160 |
| Herodotus (*History*) | 480–425 B.C. |
| Horace | |
| Sophocles | 496–406 B.C. |
| Lucretius | d. 55 or 53 B.C. |
| Catullus | 54 B.C. |
| Euripides | 480–406 B.C. |
| Demosthenes | 383–322 B.C. |
| Aristotle | 384–322 B.C. |
| Aristophanes | 450–385 B.C. |
| Homer (*Iliad*) | 900 B.C. |
| New Testament | A.D. 40–100 |

From *Evidence That Demands a Verdict*, 42-43.

Greek copies in existence that contain all or part of the New Testament in Greek. The earliest fragment dates about A.D. 120.

Two major manuscripts, Codex Vaticanus (A.D. 325) and Codex Sinaiticus (A.D. 350), a complete copy of the New Testament, date within 250 years of the original writing. That may seem like a long time span, but it is minimal compared to most ancient works. The first complete copy of the *Odyssey* is from 2,200 years after it was written!

---

## HOW DO THEY STACK UP?

| Earliest Copy | Time Span | No. of Copies |
|---|---|---|
| A.D. 900 | 1,000 yrs. | 10 |
| | | 20 |
| A.D. 900 | 1,200 yrs. | 7 |
| A.D. 1100 | 1,000 yrs. | 20 (–) |
| A.D. 1000 | 900 yrs. | 1 |
| A.D. 850 | 750 yrs. | 7 |
| A.D. 900 | 1,300 yrs. | 8 |
| A.D. 950 | 800 yrs. | 8 |
| A.D. 900 | 1,300 yrs. | 8 |
| | 900 yrs. | |
| A.D. 1000 | 1,400 yrs. | 193 |
| | 1,100 yrs. | 2 |
| A.D. 1550 | 1,600 yrs. | 3 |
| A.D. 1100 | 1,500 yrs. | 9 |
| A.D. 1100 | 1,300 yrs. | 200* |
| A.D. 1100 | 1,400 yrs. | 49** |
| A.D. 900 | 1,200 yrs. | 10 |
| 400 B.C. | 500 yrs. | 643 |
| A.D. 125 | 25 yrs. | over 24,000 |

*All from one copy. **Of any one work.

A few years ago, 36,000 *quotations* of the Scriptures by the early church fathers could be documented. But more recently, as a result of research done at the British Museum, we are now able to document 89,000 quotations from the New Testament in early church writings. If you destroyed all the Bibles and biblical manuscripts, one could reconstruct all but eleven verses of the entire New Testament from quotations found in other materials written within 150 to 200 years after the time of Jesus Christ!

These facts are called the *bibliographical* test, which determines only that the text we have now is what was originally written.

QUESTION 4: *How do we know the writers got their facts straight in the first place? Maybe it was just hearsay.*

"Hearsay" is not admissible as evidence in a court of law. *The Federal Rules of Evidence* declares that a witness must testify concerning what he has firsthand knowledge of, not what has come to him indirectly from other sources.

FACT: *The New Testament does not fit the mode of hearsay.*

Concerning the value of a person testifying of his own knowledge, Dr. John Warwick Montgomery, an attorney and dean of the Simon Greenleaf School of Law, points out that from a legal perspective, the New Testament documents meet the demand for "primary-source" evidence. He writes that the New Testament record is "fully vindicated by the constant assertions of their authors to be setting forth that which we have heard, which we have seen with our eyes, which we have looked upon and our hands have handled."[2]

FACT: *Most testimony in the New Testament comes from firsthand knowledge.*

For example, when Mary went to the tomb, the angel appeared to her and said, "He is not here, He has risen." When Mary told the disciples, it was hearsay because she hadn't seen Him herself; she just had heard about it. But later, Jesus personally appeared to Mary. That took it out of hearsay and made her testimony a primary source.

Dr. Louis Gottschalk, former professor of history at the University of Chicago, outlines his historical method in an excellent guide used by many for historical investigation. Gottschalk points out that the ability of the writer or the witness to tell the truth is helpful to the historian to determine credibility, "even if it is contained in a document obtained by force or fraud, or is otherwise impeachable, or is based on hearsay evidence, or is from an interested witness."[3]

This ability to tell the truth, Gottschalk points out, is closely related to the witness's nearness both geographically and chronologically to the events recorded.

53

What about the New Testament accounts? The New Testament accounts of the life and teachings of Jesus were recorded by men who either had been eyewitnesses themselves or who were recounting the descriptions of eyewitnesses. For instance:

- Luke wrote to Theophilus, "It seemed fitting for me as well, having investigated everything carefully from the beginning, to write it out for you in consecutive order" (Luke 1:1-3).
- Peter wrote, "We were eyewitnesses" (2 Peter 1:16).
- Wrote John, "What we have seen and heard we proclaim to you . . ." (1 John 1:3) and "his witness is true, and he knows that he is telling the truth . . ." (John 19:35).
- Luke painstakingly listed proven historical facts (Luke 3:1).

This closeness to the recorded accounts is an extremely effective means of certifying the accuracy of what is retained by a witness.

QUESTION 5: *But what if the writers simply told falsehoods?*

Good question. The historian does have to deal with the eyewitness who consciously or unconsciously tells falsehoods, even though he is near the event and is competent to tell the truth.

FACT: *The New Testament writers ap-*

*pealed to common knowledge about Jesus.*

The New Testament accounts of Christ were being circulated within the lifetimes of His contemporaries. Those people could have confirmed or denied the accuracy of the accounts. The writers not only said, "Look, we saw this" or "We heard that." But right in front of their most severe opponents they turned the tables around and said, "You also know about these things—you saw them yourselves." (One had better be careful when he says to the opposition, "You know this also," because if he isn't right in the details, he will be exposed immediately!)

Speaking to the Jewish people, Peter said, "Men of Israel, listen to these words: Jesus the Nazarene, a man attested to you by God with miracles and wonders and signs which God performed through Him" [notice this] *"in your midst, just as you yourselves know . . ."* (Acts 2:22). If they hadn't seen those miracles for themselves, Peter never would have gotten out of there alive, let alone have thousands trust in Christ.

F. F. Bruce, a professor at Manchester University, makes an astute observation in his book *The New Testament Documents— Are They Reliable?* about the value not only of friendly witnesses (those that agree with you), but also *hostile witnesses:* "The disciples could not afford to risk inaccuracies (not to speak of willful manipulation of the facts) which would at once be exposed by those who would only have been glad to do so."[4]

QUESTION 6: *So Jesus died on the cross, and later His followers were killed. But "dying for a great cause" doesn't prove the truth of that cause, does it? After all, a lot of people in history have died for great causes.*

FACT: *What the disciples thought was their "great cause" died on the cross.*

When Jesus died that Friday, the disciples no longer had a "great cause." Remember, the Jews at that time were under oppression from the Romans. To hold the allegiance of the people, the Jewish leaders taught that when the Messiah came, He would come as a reigning political Messiah, and He'd throw the Romans out.

That is why it was so hard for the apostles to understand what Jesus was saying. He said, "I have to die. I have to go to Jerusalem. I'm going to be crucified and buried." They couldn't understand it. Why? From childhood it had been ingrained into them that when the Messiah came, He would reign politically. They thought they were in on something big. They were going to rule with Him.

Professor E. F. Scott, in his book *Kingdom and the Messiah,* points out that "for the people at large, their Messiah remained what He had been to Isaiah and his contemporaries, the Son of David, who

56

would bring victory and prosperity to the Jewish nation."[5]

Dr. Jacob Gardenhus, a Jewish scholar, observed that the Jews awaited the Messiah as the One who would deliver them from Roman oppression. The temple with its sacrificial service was intact because the Romans did not interfere in Jewish religious affairs. The messianic hope was basically for national liberation, for a Redeemer of a country that was being oppressed.

*The Jewish Encyclopedia* records that the Jews "yearned for the promised Deliverer of the house of David who would free them from the yoke of the hated foreign usurper, who would put an end to the impious world and rule, and would establish His own reign of peace and justice in its place."[6]

Therefore, at the point of Jesus' crucifixion, the disciples "great cause" was dead from their natural perspective. There would have been nothing for them to die for. Their hopes were dashed.

FACT: *It was the Resurrection that totally changed the lives of the disciples.*

But then something happened. In a matter of a few days their lives were turned upside down. All but one became a martyr for the cause of the Man who appeared to them after His death. With the Resurrection they finally understood what Jesus had been saying: He had come to suffer and die for the sins of the world, and He would come a second time to reign throughout the world. The Resurrection is the only thing that could have changed those frightened, discouraged disciples into apostles who would dedicate their lives to spreading His message. Once they were convinced of it, they never denied it.

QUESTION 7: *Isn't the Bible just witnessing to itself?*

OK, so the "internal evidence" is pretty convincing that the New Testament picture of Christ can be trusted. But isn't that just the Bible being its own witness? Are there any other sources of proof?

FACT: *At least two historians of the time offer external evidence as well.*

The historian Eusebius preserves some writings of Papias, bishop of Hierapolis (A.D. 130):

The Elder [Apostle John] used to say this also: "Mark, having been the interpreter of Peter, wrote down accurately all that he [Peter] mentioned, whether sayings or doings of Christ, not, however, in order. For he was neither a hearer nor a companion of the Lord; but afterward, as I said, he accompanied Peter, who adapted his teachings as necessity required, not as though he were making a compilation of the sayings of the Lord. So then Mark made no mistake, writing down in this way some things as he mentioned them; for he paid attention to this one thing, *not to* omit anything that he had heard, nor to include any false statement among them" (emphasis added).

Another historian, Irenaeus, bishop of Lyons (A.D. 180), preserves the writings of Polycarp, bishop of Smyrna, who had been a Christian for eighty-six years and was a disciple of John the apostle:

> So firm is the ground upon which these Gospels rest, that the very heretics themselves bear witness to them, and, starting from these, each one of them endeavors to establish his own particular doctrine.

Polycarp was saying that the four Gospel accounts about what Christ said and did were so accurate (firm) that even the heretics themselves in the first century could not deny their record of events. Instead of attacking the scriptural account, which would have proven fruitless, the heretics started with the teachings of Jesus and developed their own heretical interpretations. Since they weren't able to say, "Jesus didn't say that," they instead had to say, "This is what He meant. . . ." (You are on pretty solid ground when you get those who disagree with you to do that!)

FACT: *Archaeology, too, often provides powerful external evidence.*

Archaeology contributes to biblical criticism, not in the area of inspiration and revelation, but by providing evidence of accuracy about events that are recorded. Archaeologist Joseph Free, in his book, *Archaeology and Bible History,* says that archaeology has confirmed countless biblical passages that were earlier rejected by critics as unhistorical or contradictory to supposedly "known" facts.[7]

For instance, Luke at one time was considered incorrect for referring to the Philippian rulers as *praetors.* According to the "scholars," two *duumuirs* would have ruled the town. However, Luke was right. Archaeological findings have shown the title of *praetor* was employed by the magistrates of a Roman colony.

Luke's choice of the word *proconsul* as the title for Gallio also has been proven correct, as evidenced by the Delphi inscription which states: "As Lucius Junius Gallio, my friend, and the proconsul of Achaia . . . " (compare Acts 18:12).

Again and again Luke's historical references have been substantiated. Notice that in the first verse of Luke 3 there are fifteen historical references given by Luke that can be checked for accuracy: "Now in the fifteenth year [that's one historical reference] of the reign of Tiberius Caesar [that's two], when Pontius Pilate [three] was governor [four] of Judea [five], and Herod [six] was tetrarch [seven] of Galilee [eight], and his brother Philip [nine] was tetrarch [ten] of the region of Ituraea and Trachonitis [eleven and twelve], and Lysanias [thirteen] was tetrarch [fourteen] of Abilene [fifteen] ..."

It is no wonder that E. M. Blaiklock, professor of classics at Auckland University, concludes that "Luke is a consummate historian, to be ranked in his own right with the great writers of the Greeks."

FACT: *One test of a writer is consistency.*

Commenting on the overall historical accuracy of Luke, F. F. Bruce (noted earlier) says, "A man whose accuracy can be demonstrated in matters where we are able to test it is likely to be accurate even where the means for testing him are not available. . . . Luke's record entitles him to be regarded as a writer of habitual accuracy."[9]

FACT: *The same standard or test should be applied to the Bible as is applied to secular literature.*

There was a time in my life when I myself tried to shatter the historicity and validity of the Scriptures. But I have come to the conclusion that they are historically trustworthy. If a person discards the Bible as unreliable in this sense, then he or she must discard almost all the literature of antiquity.

One problem I constantly face is the desire on the part of many to apply one standard or test to secular literature and another to the Bible. But we need to apply the same test, whether the literature under investigation is secular or religious, without incorporating presuppositions or assumptions that rule out certain content, i.e., the supernatural.

Dr. Clark Pinnock, in his book *Set Forth Your Case,* concluded after extensive research, "There exists no document from the ancient world, witnessed by so excellent a set of textual and historical testimonies and offering so superb an array of historical data on which an intelligent decision may be made. An honest person cannot dismiss a source of this kind. Skepticism regarding the historical credentials of Christianity is based upon an irrational bias."[10]

F. F. Bruce makes the following observation:

> The evidence for our New Testament writings is ever so much greater than the evidence for many writings of classical authors, the authenticity of which no one dreams of questioning. . . .[11]

And if the New Testament were a collection of secular writings, their authenticity would generally be regarded as beyond all doubt.

FACT: *The New Testament portrays historical reality.*

The late historian Will Durant, trained in the discipline of historical investigation, who spent his life analyzing records of antiquity, writes:

> Despite the prejudices and theological preconceptions of the evangelists, they

record many incidents that mere inventors would have concealed—the competition of the apostles for high places in the Kingdom, their flight after Jesus' arrest, Peter's denial, the failure of Christ to work miracles in Galilee, the references of some authors to His possible insanity, His despairing cry on the cross; no one reading these scenes can doubt the reality of the figure behind them. That a few simple men should in one generation have invented so powerful and appealing a personality, so lofty an ethic, and so inspiring a vision of human brotherhood, would be a miracle far more incredible than any recorded in the Gospels. After two centuries of Higher Criticism, the outlines of the life, character, and teachings of Christ remain reasonably clear, and constitute the most fascinating feature in the history of Western man.[12]

# *What It Means Today*

What difference does it make if the Bible is historically accurate or not? After all, a lot of people regard the Bible as good literature, like the works of Shakespeare or Aristotle.

But the historically accurate portrait of Christ in the New Testament has personal implications for everyone.

The claims that Scripture makes for itself (that it is the Word of God to us) and that Jesus makes for Himself (that He is God's Son, sent to redeem men and women and reconcile us to God) are either the biggest lies and the cruelest hoax foisted on the human race—or they are the most remarkable and noteworthy claims in history.

The birth, life, death, and resurrection of Jesus was a turning point in the history of mankind. Measured by His influence, Jesus is central to the human story.

## THE POWER OF CHRIST

The Christ of the New Testament can change lives. No matter what the critics say, the Christ of the New Testament changes lives. Millions from all backgrounds, nationalities, races, and professions, more than twenty centuries, are witnesses to the sin-breaking power of God's forgiveness through Jesus Christ.

E. Y. Mullins writes:

> A redeemed drunkard, with vivid memory of past hopeless struggles and new sense of power through Christ, was replying to the charge that his religion was a delusion. He said: "Thank God for the delusion; it has put clothes on my children and shoes on their feet and bread in their mouths. It has made a man of me and it has put joy and peace in my home, which had been hell. If this is a delusion, may God send it to the slaves of drink everywhere, for their slavery is an awful reality."[1]

I, too, am a walking testimony that the Scriptures are true, that Jesus Christ was raised from the dead and lives today.

When I was a student I set out to refute intellectually the Bible as a reliable document, the Resurrection as a factual historical event, and Christianity as a relevant alternative. After gathering the evidence, I was compelled to conclude that my arguments wouldn't stand up—that Jesus

Christ *is* exactly who He claimed to be, the Son of God.

My second year at the university I became a Christian. You've probably heard religious people talk about their "bolt of lightning." Well, nothing so dramatic happened to me, but in time there was some very observable changes.

*Mental Peace.* I had been a person who always had to be occupied. I had to be over at my girl's place or somewhere in a rap session. I'd walk across campus, and my mind would be a whirlwind of conflicts. I'd sit down and try to study or think, and I couldn't.

But in the few months after I made the decision to trust Christ, a kind of mental peace began to develop. Don't misunderstand, I'm not talking about the absence of conflict. What I found in this relationship with Jesus wasn't so much the absence of conflict as it was the ability to cope with it. I wouldn't trade this for anything in the world.

*Control of Temper.* Another area that started to change was my bad temper. I used to "blow my stack" if somebody just looked at me cross-eyed. I still have the scars from almost killing a man my first year in the university. My temper was such an integral part of me, I didn't consciously seek to change it.

Then one day after my decision to put my faith in Christ, I arrived at a crisis, only to find that my temper was gone!

*Freedom from Resentment.* I had a lot of hatred in my life. It wasn't something outwardly manifested, but there was a kind of inward grinding. I was ticked off with people, things, issues.

The one person I hated more than anyone else in the world was my father. I despised him. He was the town alcoholic. And if you're from a small town and one of your parents is an alcoholic, you know what I'm talking about.

Everybody knew. My friends would come to high school and make jokes about my father. They didn't think it bothered me. I was laughing on the outside, but let me tell you I was crying on the inside. I'd go out in the barn and find my mother lying in the manure behind the cows. She'd been knocked down by my father and couldn't get up.

About five months after I made my decision for Christ, love for my father—a love from God through Jesus Christ—inundated my life. It took that resentment and turned it upside down. It was so strong, I was able to look my father squarely in the eye and say, "Dad, I love you." I really meant it.

When I transferred to a private university, I was in a serious car accident. With my neck in traction, I was taken home. I'll never forget my father coming into my room, standing by my bed, and asking,

"Son, how can you love a father like me?"

I said, "Dad, six months ago I despised you." Then I shared with him my conclusions about Jesus Christ and how He had changed me.

Forty-five minutes later one of the greatest thrills of my life occurred. Somebody in my own family, someone who knew me so well I couldn't pull the wool over his eyes, my own father, said to me, "Son, if God can do in my life what I've seen Him do in yours, then I want to give Him the opportunity."

Usually changes take place over several days, weeks, or even years. But my father was changed right before my eyes. It was as though somebody reached in and turned on a light bulb. I've never seen such a rapid change before or since. My father touched alcohol only once after that. He got it as far as his lips, and that was it. He didn't need it any more.

I've come to one conclusion: A relationship with Jesus Christ changes people. You can ignore Him; you can mock or ridicule Christianity. It's your decision. And yet, when all else is said and done, we must face the fact that Peter pointed out: "Jesus [is] the Messiah. . . . There is salvation in no one else! Under all heaven there is no other name for men to call upon to save them" (Acts 4:11-12).

If you ask Him to take control of your life, start watching your attitudes and ac-

# The Focal Point of Christian Experience: Jesus Christ

Many people have the impression that Christian conversion is a psychologically induced experience brought about by brainwashing the subject with persuasive words and emotional presentations of Christian "myths." An evangelist is thought of as a psychologist manipulating weak, helpless minds into conformity with his own views.

Some have even suggested that the Christian experience can be explained on the basis of conditioned reflexes. They claim that anyone, after repeated exposure to Christian thought, can be caught in a type of "spiritual hypnosis," in which he will mechanically react in certain ways under certain conditions.

*Paul Little* in *Know Why You Believe* concludes that "to explain all Christian experience on a psychological basis does not fit the facts." He adds that "Christian experience can be described psychologically, but this does not explain why it happens or negate its reality."[2]

The *why* of Christian experience is the person of Jesus Christ. This fact distinguishes Christianity from all other religions, for it is only Christianity that provides a totally new source of power for living.

tions—because the Christ of the New Testament is in the business of forgiving sin,

Robert O. Ferm comments on the uniqueness of Christian conversion: "For the Christian this new center of energy is the person of Christ. The difference between the Christian and the non-Christian turns out to be, not difference in psychological symptoms, but rather in the object about which the new personality is integrated. The thing that makes Christian conversion different, then, is Christ."[3]

Furthermore, this "object" of . . . faith is not some philosophical invention of man's mind, but a physical, historical reality. . . .

The God of Christianity is not an imperceptible, unknown God, but one who has specific attributes and characteristics, which are revealed in the Scriptures. Unlike some of the religions devoted to a mystical god, Christians put their faith in a God who may be identified and who made Himself known in *history* by sending His Son, Jesus Christ. Christians can believe that their sins have been forgiven because forgiveness was accomplished and recorded in *history* by the shedding of Christ's blood on the cross. Christians can believe that Christ is now living within them because He was raised from the dead in *history*.

From *Evidence That Demands a Verdict*, 326-327.

removing guilt, changing lives, and building new relationships.

Most important of all, we can experience the power of the risen Christ in our life today.

- First, we can know the freedom of having our sins forgiven.
- Second, we can be assured of eternal life and our own resurrection from the grave.
- Third, we can be released from a meaningless and empty life and be transformed into a new creature in Jesus Christ.

WHERE DO YOU STAND?

How do you evaluate the historical evidence related in this book? What is your decision about the fact of Christ's empty tomb? *What do you think of Christ?*

When I was confronted with the overwhelming evidence for Christ's resurrection, I had to ask the logical question: "What difference does all this evidence make to me? What difference does it make whether or not I believe Christ rose again and died on the cross for my sins?"

The answer was put best by something Jesus said to a man who doubted—Thomas. He told him, "I am the Way—yes, and the Truth, and the Life. No one can get to the Father except by means of me" (John 14:6).

On the basis of all the evidence for Christ's resurrection, and considering the fact that Jesus offers forgiveness of sin and an eternal relationship with God, who would be so foolhardy as to reject Him? Christ is alive! He is living today.

You can trust God right now by faith through prayer. Prayer is talking with God. God knows your heart and is not so concerned with your words as He is with the attitude of your heart. If you have never trusted Christ, you can do so right now.

The following Four Spiritual Laws or principles have helped many to understand how to put one's trust in Christ as Savior and Lord.


## HAVE YOU HEARD OF THE FOUR SPIRITUAL LAWS?[4]

Just as there are physical laws that govern the physical universe, so there are spiritual laws that govern your relationship with God.


## LAW ONE

GOD LOVES YOU AND OFFERS A WONDERFUL PLAN FOR YOUR LIFE.

*God's Love.* "For God so loved the world, that he gave His only begotten Son, that whoever believes in Him should not perish, but have eternal life" (John 3:16).

*God's Plan.* Christ said, "I came that they might have life and might have it abundantly" (that it might be full and meaningful) (John 10:10).

Why is it that most people are not experiencing the abundant life? Because . . .

## LAW TWO

MAN IS SINFUL AND SEPARATED FROM GOD, THUS, HE CANNOT KNOW AND EXPERIENCE GOD'S LOVE AND PLAN FOR HIS LIFE.

*Man Is Sinful.* "For all have sinned and fall short of the glory of God" (Romans 3:23).

Man was created to have fellowship with God; but, because of his own stubborn self-will, he chose to go his own independent way, and fellowship with God was broken. This self-will, characterized by an attitude of active rebellion or passive indifference, is an evidence of what the Bible calls sin.

*Man Is Separated.* "For the wages of sin is death" (spiritual separation from God)

(Romans 6:23).
This diagram illustrates that God is holy and man is sinful. A great gulf separates the two. The arrows illustrate that man is continually trying to reach God and the

74

abundant life through his own efforts, such as a good life, philosophy, or religion.

The Third Law explains the only way to bridge this gulf. . . .


## LAW THREE

JESUS CHRIST IS GOD'S ONLY PROVISION FOR MAN'S SIN. THROUGH HIM YOU CAN KNOW AND EXPERIENCE GOD'S LOVE AND PLAN FOR YOUR LIFE.

*He Died in Your Place.* "But God demonstrates His own Love toward us, in that while we were yet sinners, Christ died for us" (Romans 5:8).

*He Rose from the Dead.* "Christ died for our sins . . . He was buried . . . He was raised on the third day according to the Scriptures . . . He appeared to [Peter], then to the twelve. After that he appeared to more than five hundred . . ." (1 Corinthians 15:3-6).

*He Is the Only Way to God.* "Jesus said to him, 'I am the way, and the truth, and the life; no one comes to the Father, but

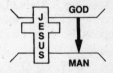

through Me'" (John 14:6).

This diagram illustrates that God has bridged the gulf which separates us from

75

Him by sending His Son, Jesus Christ, to die on the cross in our place to pay the penalty for our sins.

It is not enough to know these three laws nor even to give intellectual assent to them . . .


## LAW FOUR

WE MUST INDIVIDUALLY RECEIVE JESUS CHRIST AS SAVIOR AND LORD; THEN WE CAN KNOW AND EXPERIENCE GOD'S LOVE AND PLAN FOR OUR LIVES.

*We Must Receive Christ.* "But as many as received Him, to them He gave the right to become children of God, even to those who believe in His name" (John 1:12).

*We Receive Christ through Faith.* "For by grace you have been saved through faith; and that not of yourselves, it is the gift of God; not as a result of works, that no one should boast" (Ephesians 2:8-9).

When we receive Christ, we experience a new birth. (Read John 3:1-8.)

*We Receive Christ by Personal Invitation.* (Christ is speaking) "Behold, I stand at the door and knock; if anyone hears My voice and opens the door, I will come in to him" (Revelation 3:20).

Receiving Christ involves turning to God from self (repentance) and trusting Christ to come into our lives to forgive our sins and to make us the kind of people He wants us to be. Just to agree intellectually that Jesus Christ is the Son of God and that He died on the cross for our sins is not enough. Nor is it enough to have an emotional experience. We receive Jesus

**THESE TWO CIRCLES
REPRESENT TWO KINDS OF LIVES:**

SELF-DIRECTED LIFE
S – Self is on the throne
† – Christ is outside the life
• – Interests are directed by self, often resulting in discord and frustration

CHRIST-DIRECTED LIFE
† – Christ is in the life and on the throne
S – Self is yielding to Christ
• – Interests are directed by Christ, resulting in harmony with God's plan

Christ by faith, as an act of the will.

Which circle best represents your life?

Which circle would you like to have represent your life?

The following explains how you can receive Christ:

*You Can Receive Christ Right Now by Faith through Prayer.* (Prayer is talking with God.)

God knows your heart and is not so concerned with your words as He is with the attitude of your heart. The following is a suggested prayer.

"Lord Jesus, I need You. Thank You for dying on the cross for my sins. I open the door of my life and receive You as my Savior and Lord. Than You for forgiving my sins and giving me eternal life. Take control of the throne of my life. Make me the kind of person You want me to be."

Does this prayer express the desire of your heart?

If it does, pray this prayer right now, and Christ will come into your life, as He promised.

*How to Know That Christ Is in Your Life.* Did you receive Christ into your life? According to His promise in Revelation 3:20, where is Christ right now in relation to you? Christ said that He would come into your life. Would He mislead you? On what authority do you know that God has answered your prayer? (The trustworthiness of God Himself and His Word.)

*The Bible Promises Eternal Life to All who Receive Christ.* "And the witness is this, that God has given us eternal life, and this life is in His Son. He who has the Son has the life; he who does not have the Son of God does not have the life. These things I have written to you who believe in the name of the Son of God, in order that you may know that you have eternal life" (1 John 5:11-13).

Thank God that Christ is in your life and that He will never leave you. (See Hebrews 13:5.) You can know on the basis of His promise that Christ lives in you and that you have eternal life, from the very moment you invite Him in. He will not deceive you.

*Meet with Other Christians.* The Christian life was not meant to be lived alone. God's Word admonishes us not to forsake "the assembling of ourselves together . . ." (Hebrews 10:25). Several logs burn brightly together; but put one aside on the cold hearth and the fire goes out. So it is with your relationship to other Christians. If you do not belong to a church, do not wait to be invited. Take the initiative; call the pastor of a nearby church where Christ is honored and His Word is preached. Start this week, and make plans to attend regularly.

*Special Materials Are Available for Christian Growth.* If you have established a relationship with God through Christ as you were reading the above, please write me and tell me about it. I would be delighted to send you some materials that will help you in your ongoing walk with God.

Josh McDowell
Box 1000
Dallas, TX 75221

# The Bible—
# Why It's Unique

A representative of the *Great Books of the Western World* came to my house recruiting salesmen for their series. He spread out the chart of the *Great Books of the Western World* series. He spent five minutes talking to us about the *Great Books of the Western World* series, and we spent an hour and a half talking to him about the Greatest Book.

I challenged him to take just ten of the authors, all from one walk of life, one generation, one place, one time, one mood, one continent, one language, and just one controversial subject (the Bible speaks on hundreds with harmony and agreement).

Then I asked him: "Would they [the authors] agree?" He paused and then replied, "No!" "What would you have?" I retorted. Immediately he said, "A conglomeration."

Two days later he committed his life to

Christ (the theme of the Bible).

Why all this? Very simple! Any person sincerely seeking truth would at least consider a book with the following unique qualifications. Here is a book:

1. Written over a 1,500 year span.

2. Written over forty generations.

3. Written by more than forty authors from every walk of life, including kings, peasants, philosophers, fishermen, poets, statesmen, and scholars.

Among its authors were Moses, a political leader trained in the universities of Egypt; Peter, a fisherman; Joshua, a military general; Nehemiah, a cupbearer; Daniel, a prime minister; Luke, a doctor; Matthew, a tax collector; Paul, a rabbi.

4. Written on three continents: Asia, Africa, and Europe

5. Written in three languages: Hebrew, the language of the Old Testament; Aramaic, the "common language" of the Near East until the time of Alexander the Great (6th–4th century B.C.); Greek, the language of the New Testament.

6. Treating hundreds of controversial subjects with harmony and continuity from Genesis to Revelation. (A controversial subject is one that would create opposing opinions when mentioned or discussed.) There is one unfolding story: "God's redemption of man."

Geisler and Nix put it this way: "The 'Paradise Lost' of the Genesis becomes the 'Paradise Regained' of Revelation. Whereas the gate to the tree of life is closed in Genesis, it is opened forevermore in Revelation."[1]

F. F. Bruce concludes: "The Bible, at first sight, appears to be a collection of literature—mainly Jewish. If we inquire into the circumstances under which the various biblical documents were written, we find that they were written at intervals over a space of nearly 1400 years. The writers wrote in various lands, from Italy in the west to Mesopotamia and possibly Persia in the east. The writers themselves were a heterogeneous number of people, not only separated from each other by hundreds of years and hundreds of miles, but belonging to the most diverse walks of life. In their ranks we have kings, herdsmen, soldiers, legislators, fishermen, statesmen, courtiers, priests and prophets, a tentmaking rabbi, and a Gentile physician, not to speak of others of whom we know nothing apart from the writings they have left us. The writings themselves belong to a great variety of literary types. They include history, law (civil, criminal, ethical, ritual, sanitary), religious poetry, didactic treatises, lyric poetry, parable and allegory, biography, personal correspondence, personal memoirs and diaries, in addition to the distinctively biblical types of prophecy and apocalyptic.

"For all that, the Bible is not simply an

anthology; there is a unity which binds the whole together. An anthology is compiled by an anthologist, but no anthologist compiled the Bible."[2]

From *Evidence That Demands a Verdict*, 16-17.

# Jesus Christ— Was He Messiah?

The following Old Testament predictions about the Messiah were literally fulfilled in Christ.

HIS FIRST ADVENT

*The fact.* Genesis 3:15; Deuteronomy 18:15; Psalm 89:20; Isaiah 9:6; 28:16; 32:1; 35:4; 42:6; 49:1; 55:4; Ezekiel 34:24; Daniel 2:44; Micah 4:1; Zechariah 3:8.

*The time.* Genesis 49:10; Numbers 24:17; Daniel 9:24; Malachi 3:1.

*His divinity.* Psalm 2:7, 11; 45:6-7, 11; 72:8; 102:24-27; 89:26-27; 110:1; Isaiah 9:6; 25:9; 40:10; Jeremiah 23:6; Micah 5:2; Malachi 3:1.

*Human generation.* Genesis 12:3; 18:18; 21:12; 22:18; 26:4; 28:14; 49:10; 2 Samuel 7:14; Psalm 18:4-6, 50; 22:22-23; 89:4; 29:36; 132:11; Isaiah 11:1; Jeremiah 23:5; 33:15.

## HIS FORERUNNER
Isaiah 40:3; Malachi 3:1; 4:5.


## HIS NATIVITY AND EARLY YEARS
*The fact.* Genesis 3:15; Isaiah 7:14; Jeremiah 31:22.

*The place.* Numbers 24:17, 19; Micah 5:2.

*Adoration by Magi.* Psalm 72:10, 15; Isaiah 60:3, 6.

*Descent into Egypt.* Hosea 11:1.

*Massacre of innocents.* Jeremiah 31:15.


## HIS MISSION AND OFFICE
*Mission.* Genesis 12:3; 49:10; Numbers 24:19; Deuteronomy 18:18-19; Psalm 21:1; Isaiah 59:20; Jeremiah 33:16.

*Priest like Melchizedek.* Psalm 110:4.

*Prophet like Moses.* Deuteronomy 18:15.

*Conversion of Gentiles.* Isaiah 11:10; Deuteronomy 32:43; Psalm 18:49; 19:4; 117:1; Isaiah 42:1; 45:23; 49:6; Hosea 1:10; 2:23; Joel 2:32.

*Ministry in Galilee.* Isaiah 9:1-2.

*Miracles.* Isaiah 35:5-6; 42:7; 53:4.

*Spiritual graces.* Psalm 45:7; Isaiah 11:2; 42:1; 53:9; 61:1-2.

*Preaching.* Psalm 2:7; 78:2; Isaiah 2:3; 61:1; Micah 4:2.

*Purification of the temple.* Psalm 69:9.

# HIS PASSION

*Rejection by Jews and Gentiles.* Psalm 2:1; 22:12; 41:5; 56:5; 69:8; 118:22-23; Isaiah 6:9-10; 8:14; 29:13; 53:1; 65:2.

*Persecution.* Psalm 22:6; 35:7, 12; 56:5; 71:10; 109:2; Isaiah 49:7; 53:3.

*Triumphal entry into Jerusalem.* Psalm 8:2; 118:25-26; Zechariah 9:9.

*Betrayal by a friend.* Psalm 41:9; 55:13; Zechariah 13:6.

*Betrayal for thirty pieces of silver.* Zechariah 11:12.

*Betrayer's death.* Psalm 55:15, 23; 109:17.

*Purchase of potter's field.* Zechariah 11:13.

*Desertion by disciples.* Zechariah 13:7.

*False accusation.* Psalm 27:12; 35:11; 109:2.

*Silence under accusation.* Psalm 38:13; Isaiah 53:7.

*Mocking.* Psalm 22:7-8, 16; 109:25.

*Insult, buffeting, spitting, scourging.* Psalm 35:15, 21; Isaiah 50:6.

*Patience under suffering.* Isaiah 53:7-9.

*Crucifixion.* Psalm 22:14, 17.

*Offer of gall and vinegar.* Psalm 69:21.

*Prayer for enemies.* Psalm 109:4.

*Cries upon the cross.* Psalm 22:1; 31:5.

*Death in prime of life.* Psalm 89:45; 102:24.

*Death with malefactors.* Isaiah 53:9, 12.

*Death attested by convulsions of nature.* Amos 5:20; Zechariah 14:4, 6.

*Casting of lots for clothing.* Psalm 22:18.

*Bones left unbroken.* Psalm 34:20.

*Piercing.* Psalm 22:16; Zechariah 12:10; 13:6.

*Voluntary death.* Psalm 40:6-8.

*Vicarious suffering.* Isaiah 53:4-6, 12; Daniel 9:26.

*Burial with the rich.* Isaiah 53:9.


## HIS RESURRECTION
Psalm 16:8-10; 30:3; 41:10; 118:17; Hosea 6:2.


## HIS ASCENSION
Psalm 16:11; 24:7; 68:18; 110:1; 118:19.


## HIS SECOND COMING
Psalm 50:3-6; Isaiah 9:6-7; 66:18; Daniel 7:13-14; Zechariah 12:10; 14:4-8.


## DOMINION UNIVERSAL AND EVERLASTING
1 Chronicles 17:11-14; Psalm 2:6-8; 8:6; 45:6-7; 72:8; 110:1-3; Isaiah 9:7; Daniel 7:14.

From *Evidence That Demands a Verdict,* 175-176.

# *Notes*

INTRODUCTION
1. William E. Lecky, *History of European Morals from Augustus to Charlemagne* (New York: D. Appleton and Co., 1903), 2:8-9.
2. J. T. Fisher, and L. S. Hawley, *A Few Buttons Missing* (New York: MacMillan, 1947), 113.

CHAPTER 1
1. William F. Albright, *Recent Discoveries in Bible Lands* (New York: Funk and Wagnalls, 1955), 136.
2. Sir Frederick Kenyon, *The Bible and Archaeology* (New York: Harper and Row, 1940), 288-289.
3. Sir William Ramsay, *The Bearing of Recent Discovery on the Trustworthiness of the New Testament* (London: Hodder and Stoughton, 1915), 222.
4. F. F. Bruce, *The New Testament Documents: Are They Reliable?* rev. ed. (Grand Rapids, Mich.: Eerdmans, 1977), 33.
5. J. N. D. Anderson, *Christianity: The Witness of History* (Wheaton, Ill.: Tyndale, 1970), 92.
6. John Warwick Montgomery, *History and Christianity* (Downers Grove, Ill.: InterVarsity Press, 1972), 78.
7. David Friedrich Strauss, *The Life of Jesus for the People*, 2d ed. (London: Williams and Norgate, 1879), 1:412.

8. Gaston F. Poote, *The Transformation of the Twelve* (Nashville, Tenn.: Abingdon, 1958), 12.
9. Michael Green, "Editor's Preface" in George Eldon Ladd, *I Believe in the Resurrection of Jesus* (Grand Rapids, Mich.: Eerdmans, 1975).

CHAPTER 2

1. Paul Althaus, *Die Wahrheit des kirchlichen Osterglaubens* (Gütersloh: C. Bertelsmann, 1941), 22, 25ff.
2. George Currie, *The Military Discipline of the Romans from the Founding of the City to the Close of the Republic.* An abstract of a thesis published under the auspices of the Graduate Council of Indiana University, 1928, 41-43.
3. Thomas Arnold, *Christian Life—Its Hopes, Its Fears, and Its Close,* 6th ed. (London: T. Fellowes, 1859), 324.

CHAPTER 3

1. John A. T. Robinson, *Time* (21 March 1977), 95.
2. John Warwick Montgomery, "Legal Reasoning and Christian Apologetics," *The Law Above the Law* (Chicago: Christian Legal Society, 1975), 88-89.
3. Louis R. Gottschalk, *Understanding History,* 2d ed. (New York: Knopf, 1969), 150.
4. Bruce, *The New Testament Documents,* 33.
5. Earnest Findlay Scott, *Kingdom and the Messiah* (Edinburgh: T and T Clark, 1911), 55.
6. *The Jewish Encyclopedia* (New York: Funk and Wagnalls, 1906), 8:508.
7. Joseph Free, *Archaeology and Bible History* (Wheaton, Ill.: Scripture Press, 1969), 1.
8. E. M. Blaiklock, *The Acts of the Apostles* (Grand Rapids, Mich.: Eerdmans, 1959), 89.
9. Josh McDowell, *The Resurrection Factor* (San Bernardino, Calif.: Here's Life Publishers, 1981), 34-35.
10. Clark Pinnock, *Set Forth Your Case* (New Jersey: The Craig Press, 1968), 68.
11. Bruce, *The New Testament Documents,* 15.
12. Will Durant, *Caesar and Christ, the Story of*

*Civilization* (New York: Simon and Schuster, 1944), 3:557.

CHAPTER 4
1. Josh McDowell, *Evidence That Demands a Verdict* (San Bernardino, Calif.: Here's Life Publishers, 1979), 328.
2. Paul Little, *Know Why You Believe* (Wheaton, Ill.: Scripture Press, 1967), 178.
3. Robert O. Ferm, *The Psychology of Christian Conversion* (Westwood, N.J.: Fleming H. Revell, 1959), 225.
4. Written by Bill Bright. Copyright 1965 by Campus Crusade for Christ, Inc. All rights reserved.

APPENDIX 1
1. Norman L. Geisler and William E. Nix, *A General Introduction to the Bible* (Chicago: Moody Press, 1968), 24.
2. F. F. Bruce, *The Books and the Parchments,* rev. ed. (Westwood, N.J.: Fleming H. Revell, 1963), 88.

# Recommended Reading

Anderson, J. N. D. *Christianity: A Witness of History.* Downers Grove, Ill.: InterVarsity Press, 1970.

Bruce, F. F. *The New Testament Documents: Are They Reliable?* Downers Grove, Ill.: InterVarsity Press, 1964.

Free, Joseph. *Archaeology and Bible History.* Wheaton, Ill.: Scripture Press, 1969.

Henry, Carl, ed. *Revelation and the Bible.* Grand Rapids, Mich.: Baker Book House, 1969.

Latourette, Kenneth Scott. *A History of Christianity.* New York: Harper & Row, 1953.

Lewis, C. S. *Mere Christianity.* New York: Macmillan, 1952.

McDowell, Josh. *Evidence That Demands a Verdict.* San Bernardino, Calif.: Here's Life Publishers, 1986.

Montgomery, John Warwick. *History and Christianity.* Downers Grove, Ill.: InterVarsity Press, 1972.

Stott, J. R. W. *Basic Christianity.* Downers Grove, Ill.: InterVarsity Press, 1971.

*About the Author*

JOSH McDOWELL is one of the most popular speakers on the world scene today. In the last twenty-three years he has given more than 18,000 talks to more than 8 million students and faculty at 1,000 universities and high schools in seventy-two countries. Josh is author of thirty-two best-selling books and has been featured in twenty-seven films and videos and two TV specials.

Josh graduated cum laude from Kellogg College in economics and business. He finished graduate school magna cum laude with degrees in languages and theology. He is a member of two national honor societies and was selected by the Jaycees in 1976 as one of the "Outstanding Young Men in America." He holds honorary doctorate degrees in law and theology.

Josh and his wife, Dottie, have four children and live in Julian, California.

# POCKET GUIDES
## FROM TYNDALE

• **The Best Way to Plan Your Day** by Edward Dayton and Ted Engstrom. With the guidelines in this book, you can learn to effectively set goals, determine priorities, and beat the time crunch. 72-0373-1

• **Christianity: Hoax or History?** by Josh McDowell. Was Jesus Christ a liar, a lunatic, or Lord? A popular speaker and author looks at the resurrection of Jesus and other claims of the Christian faith. 72-0367-7

• **Demons, Witches, and the Occult** by Josh McDowell and Don Stewart. Why are people fascinated with the occult? This informative guide will answer your questions about occult practices and their dangers. 72-0541-6

• **Family Budgets That Work** by Larry Burkett. Customize a budget for your household with the help of this hands-on workbook. By the host of the radio talk show "How to Manage Your Money." 72-0829-6

• **Getting Out of Debt** by Howard L. Dayton, Jr. At last, a no-nonsense approach to your money problems. Here's advice on creating a budget, cutting corners, making investments, and paying off loans. 72-1004-5

• **Make Your Dream Come True** by Charles Swindoll. These ten inspirational chapters will lead any man or woman in the quest for inner strength and growth and help develop great character traits. 72-7007-2

• **Preparing for Childbirth** by Debra Evans. Expectant moms can replace their fears about childbirth with joyful anticipation. Includes suggestions that will benefit both mothers and fathers. 72-4917-0

• **Raising Teenagers Right** by James Dobson. Dr. Dobson, an authority on child development, answers some of the most-asked questions about the teenage years: how to implement discipline, build confidence, and discuss puberty. 72-5139-6

# POCKET GUIDES
## FROM TYNDALE

- **Sex, Guilt & Forgiveness** by Josh McDowell. This book offers practical counsel on learning to forgive oneself and others following sexual experiences outside of marriage. 72-5908-7

- **Six Attitudes for Winners** by Norman Vincent Peale. Let an internationally known speaker and author help you replace fear, worry, apathy, and despair with courage, peace, hope, and enthusiasm. 72-5906-0

- **Skeptics Who Demanded a Verdict** by Josh McDowell. Three convincing stories of faith from some famous skeptics: C.S. Lewis, Charles Colson, and Josh McDowell. 72-5925-7

- **Temper Your Child's Tantrums** by James Dobson. You don't need to feel frustrated as a parent. The celebrated author and "Focus on the Family" radio host wants to give you the keys to firm, but loving, discipline in your home. 72-6994-5

- **Terrific Tips for Parents** by Paul Lewis. The editor of DADS ONLY newsletter shares his findings on building character, confidence, and closeness at home. 72-7010-2